ColorMaps™

GARDEN

1 2 3 4 5 6 COLOR-CODED PATTERNS 7 8 9 10 11 12

Illustrated by
Olivia Gibbs

BETTER DAY BOOKS™
HAPPY · CREATIVE · CURATED™

© Olivia Gibbs

6

© Olivia Gibbs

7

© Olivia Gibbs

© Olivia Gibbs

ColorMaps™ Garden

© Olivia Gibbs

© Olivia Gibbs

to PLANT a GARDEN is to believe in TOMORROW

medicinal HERBS

evening primrose

dandelion

chamomile

mint

rosemary

lavender

medicinal HERBS

evening primrose

dandelion

chamomile

mint

rosemary

lavender

| 1 | 2 | | 4 | 5 | | | 9 | 10 | | 12 |

© Olivia Gibbs

23

© Olivia Gibbs

© Olivia Gibbs

30 © Olivia Gibbs

 © Olivia Gibbs

a Garden FEEDS the SOUL

© Olivia Gibbs

© Olivia Gibbs

© Olivia Gibbs

© Olivia Gibbs

© Olivia Gibbs

 © Olivia Gibbs

© Olivia Gibbs

46

© Olivia Gibbs

49

© Olivia Gibbs

© Olivia Gibbs

© Olivia Gibbs

Life BEGINS in a GARDEN

Bonus Patterns

Sometimes once just isn't enough!
In the following pages, you will have a second
chance to color each of the patterns from
the front of this book. Have fun recoloring
your favorite designs or pair up with a buddy
and color together. It's up to you!

64

© Olivia Gibbs

72

© Olivia Gibbs

medicinal HERBS

evening primrose

dandelion

chamomile

mint

rosemary

lavender

| 1 | 2 | | 4 | 5 | | | 9 | 10 | | 12 |

© Olivia Gibbs

74

© Olivia Gibbs

75

© Olivia Gibbs

© Olivia Gibbs

© Olivia Gibbs

BETTER DAY BOOKS™
HAPPY · CREATIVE · CURATED™

Business is personal at Better Day Books. We were founded on the belief that all people are creative and that making things by hand is inherently good for us. It's important to us that you know how much we appreciate your support. The book you are holding in your hands was crafted with the artistic passion of the author and brought to life by a team of wildly enthusiastic creatives who believed it could inspire you. If it did, please drop us a line and let us know about it. Connect with us on Instagram, post a photo of your art, and let us know what other creative pursuits you are interested in learning about. It all matters to us. You're kind of a big deal.

it's a good day to have a better day!™

www.betterdaybooks.com

better_day_books

If you like this book, please check out the full line of ColorMaps™ coloring books at www.betterdaybooks.com